Echoes of Tradition

An Anthology
Tulsa NightWriters

Tulsa NightWriters

ISBN: 979-8-218-58176-3

Edited by Aubrey Green and Madeleine Kepros

A very special thank you to our editors, Aubrey Green and Madeleine Kepros, for their dedication and hard work on this anthology.

Contents

Introduction

by J. D. Colbert

Echoes of Tradition:
Indigenous Orientation to
Community, Time, and Land
an Anthology

McGirt.

With the U.S. Supreme Court's decision in McGirt v. Oklahoma (2020), Oklahoma's complex, tortured, and extensive relationship with tribal nations suddenly became front-page news worldwide.

The announcement riveted the general public. The McGirt case reanimated one hundred plus years old treaties and agreements going back to the founding of the state of Oklahoma. More than the legalities, it was the Native culture, traditional governance, and lifeways imbued in the court's decision that garnered the public's attention.

People eagerly researching the political/legal history quickly encountered an Indigenous culture whose values, polity, and relationship to Mother Earth stand in stark contrast to that of Western Society today. Researchers correctly surmised that to understand the McGirt decision fully, they had to attain a better comprehension of Native peoples and their societies.

Enter the Tulsa NightWriters. As we at Tulsa NightWriters were preparing for this, our third anthology, the first order of business, was to select a theme. With the public's thirst for Indigenous knowledge unabated, it was clear that our theme should encompass McGirt, not in its legal context but rather from an anthropological, sociological, and historical perspective.

Accordingly, we settled upon the theme of "Echoes of Tradition: Indigenous Orientation to Community, Time, and Land." Within these pages, you'll find Native viewpoints and stories that manifest notable difference in the understanding of community, time, and land. With regard to community, for example, you'll find selections that draw stark distinctions in Native societies that emphasize the overall community good versus individual rights.

It is our hope that this anthology will better ground the reader into the unique worldview of Native societies and thereby better understand the McGirt decision beyond its immediate political/legal dimensions. Indeed, with the insightful contributions of the talented authors at Tulsa NightWriters, our highest aspiration is that you might see your own world through a new lens, a Red Lens, and thus know the familiar in a deeper, richer way.

And now, as you stand at the threshold of delving into this delicious and educational cornucopia of literary excellence brought to you by the Tulsa NightWriters, I ask you to please click your heels together three times and repeat after me, "McGirt, McGirt, McGirt."

****

Echoes of Tradition: Indigenous Orientation to Community, Time and Land is an anthology that was produced under the guidance of the nonprofit Tulsa NightWriters, one of Oklahoma's oldest writing organizations. It has been in existence since 1957 and welcomes writers of all ages, regardless of their preferred genre or level of experience. For more information about meetings, conferences, events, and other gatherings, please visit our website at tulsanightwriters.org.

501c3 #47-5492695

By the Creek

by Margaret Lee

Can a thin stream, swollen

by the storm,

lead me back

to the source

of this water,

this people, called *Creek*

because they made home

on banks where

river birch and jewelweed

knew their names?

Not confined

to a house

of rivercane and thatch.

Not restricted to one town.

Home was any dwelling

of a member of the clan:

each Fox at home

with every other Fox,

Skunk with Skunk, Wind with Wind.

Not a place,

a network—lily pads connected

underwater, the white globes

of a buttonbush.

But I live by lines

that make your lawn yours,

my lawn mine, a chess board

where one pawn

owns each square—

gardens of transplants.

When the taproot is cut,

the fragrance dies

with the sassafras.

Birch Tree

by Lora Lee Richmond

Peace be ever, peace be still, peace is with us now to feel. How can we make a difference in this world? To not just please us but to please all.

All that grows tall. All among us that are small. All in this field, in this park and in this lake. How much peace will it take?

The birch to some is just a weed. It is a rough nuisance that lounges by the creek to feed. In this moment we can feel the soft wood as the birch bark has peeled. The bark gone exposing the vulnerability. There is beauty that lies underneath. We too can learn from the birch tree with observation and belief.

Green Country

by Lora Lee Richmond

The green country, the old oak trees, the vines growing
on the fence next to me. The milk jug is below. The ants
work as hard as the day is long. In a row they will follow.
Maybe it's because my bare feet touch the red dirt clay as
I am alone in the Osage Hills far away. Maybe it's because
the sweetest buds are produced by the harshest soil. Decay
nourishes the juicy berries, rich dandelion wine and black
oil.

I feel every season, every touch of sun kissed light. Every
wistful wave of the wind during the night with delight.
The hottest sun beating down on my freckled face. Making
me squint my eyes and causing my redneck and flushed
face.

It's so refreshing with the blessings to come. As the light
calms down. The fireflies will jump and hum. The lessons
we learned as we played at the pool, in the lake or worked
at the watering space. That is my mother's place.

I feel the crisp refreshing autumn air and the bitter coldness of winter's ware. A touch of spring on my nose and sometimes a sudden change in the air. With a surprise storm coming up but not in despair.

This place I call home has every element I need. I can soak my feet in the cloudy, muddy lake indeed. I can skip a stone over that orange pond. I can pick the most beautiful wildflowers. Drying them upside down. Carefully not getting pollen on my pillow. The sharp arrowheads are little. They might slice your toes playing in the spring that runs in the sand. You never know what you might find on this land.

Dancing in the soft river beds below. Fossils sneak up out of the flow. Feathers of hawks and eagles are a gift. They hide on the levee banks and in the thick. The bountiful deer run and play. Shedding their antlers, bones and teeth. All that is sacred to this place underneath.

This is where I have always lived and this is where I shall stay. I couldn't possibly think of going too far away.

Brother Turtle Flies South

by Merle Davenport

In the days before Oneida warriors followed the deer, or their women planted corn, the turtle still carried his home on his back and the geese still flew south before the winter snows. Brother Bear had his winter cave and Brother Beaver his lodge, but Brother Turtle had not yet learned to bury himself in the mud until the flowers returned in the spring.

In those days, Turtle found nourishment under the snow where his short legs kept him close to the pine needles and withered grasses. When the winds blew and the wolf hunted, Brother Turtle withdrew into his home until the winds calmed and the wolf grew tired of trying to break inside. Turtle watched each summer as Brothers Beaver and Muskrat labored to build their lodges.

"Why don't you learn to carry your lodge with you?" asked Turtle as Beaver was busy chewing through a quivering aspen. "You have to carry your branches over the hill to your lodge while I can go where I please."

"You talk too much," complained Beaver. "Besides, with those short legs, how far can you go?"

"I go as far as I please," answered Turtle.

"Then why don't you fly south with the geese this winter," mocked Beaver. "Maybe if you asked, they would loan you a few feathers for your journey."

Laughing at his joke, Beaver went back to chewing down his aspen tree.

Turtle turned away. Little did Beaver know that it had always been the desire of his heart to fly south with geese. He would even give up his fine house if he could fly. Perhaps Grandfather Owl could think of a way for him to fly south.

"Grandfather, Grandfather," called Turtle when he reached Owl's home in the ancient oak.

"What is it, Brother Turtle?" asked Owl, irritated that his morning nap was interrupted.

"I want to fly south with the geese this winter," pleaded Turtle. "I would even give up my fine house if I had to."

"You talk too much," grumbled Grandfather Owl. "Go ask Sister Goose to carry you. I'm staying here to chase mice this winter."

Turtle sighed. It would take his short legs all day to reach the nest of Sister Goose. Then he remembered that her nest was at the edge of the river. Perhaps he would spend some time by the river. He could find a fallen tree and bask in the sun before jumping into the water for a cool summer swim.

"Sister Goose, Sister Goose," called Turtle when he saw Goose teaching her goslings how to fish in the river.

"What is it, Brother Turtle?" asked Goose, trying to watch her children while she talked to Turtle.

"I want to go south with you this winter," explained Turtle. "Can you carry me?"

"You talk too much," answered Goose. "You would fall long before we got there."

"I promise not to say a word if you will carry me with you," answered Turtle, excited that he might have the chance to fly south.

"Not a word?" questioned Goose, a doubtful look on her face.

"I promise," Turtle assured her. "Not a single sound."

"It would be worth the burden of carrying you just to see if you can keep silent for that long," responded Goose with a laugh. "Be here when the first leaf falls and I will carry you."

"I will. I will," Turtle promised with great enthusiasm.

When the warm winds passed and the world was preparing for winter snows, Turtle was waiting by the river. He had told everyone that he was flying south with the geese. To his surprise, no one believed he could stay quiet that long. Turtle assured all his friends that he was able to stay quiet for the entire journey.

"Brother Turtle, we have agreed to carry you, but the trip will take many days and you can't say a single word the entire way," explained Brother Goose. "Do you think you can stay quiet for that long?"

"I can," promised Turtle.

"Then bite down hard on this stick and remember, not a single word," added Sister Goose.

"This will be easy for me," replied Turtle. "Once I bite down, I won't let go."

"Remember, not one word," warned Brother Goose.

Turtle bit down hard on the stick and waited. Brother and Sister Goose each grasped one end of the stick with their feet and soared into the sky. Turtle was so surprised when his feet left the ground, he almost let go, but he remembered to bite down harder at the last moment.

Turtle could feel the wind in his face as they rose above the tallest tree. When they passed through a wet cloud, he grinned, but didn't let go. When he glanced down, he could see the tops of the trees.

"*My, how different they look from up here*," he thought. "*And look, there was a herd of deer in the clearing right next to a blue ribbon.*"

He wasn't quite sure what the ribbon was.

"The river!" he shouted to Brother and Sister Goose.

As soon as he opened his mouth, to tell Goose about the river, he fell. He couldn't bite down on the stick and talk at the same time.

Down he plunged right into the soft mud on the riverbank. He landed so hard that the mud swallowed him up. And there he stayed until the winter snows had passed. He was too embarrassed to crawl out during the long winter snows. He would not let Brother Beaver tell him that he talked too much.

From that day on, Brother Turtle has not said a word. He decided that he talked too much. Every winter, he digs a hole in the mud to hide. He no longer dreams of flying south in the winter. He is content to carry his house into the mud and stay there until the winter winds have passed.

Pillars of Power

by Gregory Bigler

Distant cities submersed in power and despair filled with
pinstriped people. Pinstriped people parading through
the city's marbled pillars. Pillars of power supporting
glistening halls using jurisprudence to fill upside-down
pyramids.

We in our overalls and ribbon-skirts dance in the night.
Our sacred fire filled with elders' embers luminate our
square-grounds hidden off the paved highways. Flames
burning yet for those clad in tee-shirts and dance-skirts,
unseen by cars rushing by at seventy-miles an-hour.

Pinstriped orators in smooth-floored corridors conjuring
into existence their jurisprudential worlds. Brick and
marble-laden buildings filled with the odorless stench
of power. Inverted pyramid creators believing the
wrong-way apex connects them to our past, neither
noticing nor caring its weight strains to break our
world.

Below pinstriped people's feet murmuring rivulets
of revenant languages flow unnoticed, their empty

eyes blind to our shadow worlds as we dance
through the night, red-flamed logs whispering to those
unseen. Conference consultants extolling old ways but
unhearing the fire burning in the dark. The glowing
sparks spiral into the evening as our songs bear witness
to our existence.

Elders' songs live within the dancing flames, stories of
our people carry prayers as they rise in the night.
Turtle shells and sweat stained tee-shirts fanning the
swirling smoke, perfuming our clothes with generations
of hickory scented memories. The twisting flames tying
worlds together, counterclockwise whirls of people,
smoke, and wind instantiating the power of life.

Overalls and jean-clad boots quietly hear in the night those
speeches angrily uttered in distant pillars of power.
Listening to the echoes of pin-striped words, then with
a shrug continue around the fire. This gift of dance
confirming our covenant with Creator.

Yet the cold stone pillars remain eternally immune to
the pull of the dancing flames. Dead words uttered
in a sea of marble tumble like a carcass down a river
that everyone sees but no one claims. Their profane
pronouncements without cadence, lifelessly held aloft
and celebrated as if a savior for us that need no salvation.

Great marbled halls lined with dead peoples' pictures
where pillar people echo things they read on parchment
papers. Paper documents written by people who debate

what others do. People in gleaming halls and oak lined rooms with vermillion curtains believing if only others paid attention the upside-down pyramids would save us all.

Pinstriped words millennium long juris-dance, plodding from parchment to paper to marbled halls, echoing lifelessly but with relentless power now dressed in suits of digital ones and zeros. Like Dr Frankenstein creating an ethereal monster. Digital monsters dance in realms unseen, unseen because the realm of ones and zeros have no spirit. The digital purveyor's progeny never able to perceive the elders' embers. At least the doctor's misunderstood creature wandered the world in tormented realization of its own blasphemy.

Digital ones and zeros stealing our songs as they used to steal our children. But these eternal pinstripe pyramids can never die because they are not alive, needing undead zombie Indians to support the upside-down edifice.

Memory filled logs burn on the red-clay hill as tree frogs sing answer our songs. Our songs forever embedded within the rings of trees that stand watch listening to dances flowing from past to present to the other side and back again. Embers burn to ash revealing Grandfather's white hair, his hair waiting contentedly till we dance again.

Colonnades of pinstriped power never knowing this land remembers us in the echo of our songs and the slow dance of trees, because upside down pyramids can never hear things they did not see in the smoke-filled night.

Lela's Gray Hair

by J B Nicholson Hunt

My small hands clutched her hairbrush
she unwound her gray bun
from combs made of bone.

Her softest smiles reserved for me
Alone with her in this quiet time
Dressing table carved by her husband.

Lela never cut her hair
And never explained her grandmother's tradition.

Her only granddaughter, I alone saw the glory.

Small pillows of hair collected from her brush
Tucked into drawers I couldn't reach.
Was it a totem? Taught by her father?
Dawes Roll #141.
His photograph on the wall.

Her strength beyond understanding
Stories left untold.

In the old photos, her hair looks shiny and soft.

I wondered if it would break
as she sometimes seemed she would.

Only a child, I couldn't know she'd had another husband
Not the man I called Grandfather.

She was an over-the-hill 25-year-old
Born near Sparks, Indian Territory.

Charley took her away from her farm work
And her half-dozen half-siblings
To a smaller farm too far for them to visit.

Her labor there was no easier
A factory worker's wife
In the darkness before electricity came home.

Sewing his clothes and hers
Intricate embroidery under dim lamplight
After long days of ironing for the bankers and lawyers

They had a son.
A year passed.
They prepared him for a baby sister.

They grew food for the table
And it was food that killed their third child
Was there no money for fresh milk?

Or maybe all their milk
Was unpasteurized, an innocent gamble
Direct from a neighbor's farm.
Too-often deadly rather than nourishing.

The factory work killed her husband.
Two children weren't quite grown.

Lela's grief held her captive
Held her apart
Held her back.

Her too-young father.
Her baby.
Her husband.

Making their own escapes
Her daughter, and then her son,
Through marriage, military service and moves.

We never talked about grandma's sad eyes
Or her father's language.
She kept her pain
on a shelf I couldn't reach.

Embers

by Lora Lee Richmond

I would rather be stunned by the ugly truth than be mesmerized by a beautiful lie. In the fall all things wither and die. We cannot stoke the flames if we are merely playing in the embers. Decay sets in nine days past December. Do everything with love and at the end of the day your heart will be full, your soul will be light and your mind will be at ease. By the springtime nature goes as wild as it may please.

I determine my worth. Not an external person or not an external circumstance. It's me. Not a past history. Not a parent that failed you. Not a sibling that betrayed you. Not whatever the hell your last relationship was. You define you.

Good love gives back. It never makes you feel like you are in want. Tell me what's worse? To be alone and feel good about yourself or be with someone and feel alone?

Find peace within yourself and get back to being you and celebrating yourself once more. How far can a connection really take you when you do most of the work yourself? The best revenge you will ever have is to not feel anything at all.

You're too busy living a life that's yours and only yours. There will be a day when I will not think of this person anymore. Stop robbing yourself of your own happiness. You are breaking your own heart. It's me that I must love because I am a piece of art. It's in the summer that we get a strong and bold start. As the sun rays beams down and we can feel the warmth. Nothing will ever tear our shining soul apart.

Little People

by Kathryn Helstrom

Author note: the names of the people involved have been changed for privacy.

Many of my students are Indian, mostly from the Muscogee Creek tribe. I use the word "Indian" because that is what my students prefer to be called. The initials NDN appear on their backpacks, clothing, and shoes. Sometimes they are written in Sharpie. Sometimes they are embroidered by their moms or grandmas. Sometimes they are beaded onto baseball caps.

So, when we launched into a project celebrating Native American Month, naturally they were proud to present some aspect of their heritage. Cole, a particularly bright and gregarious young man, was having difficulty narrowing down the specific topic he would use for his project. We sat at my desk and discussed different ideas. Marriage and folklore were two things in which he seemed to be interested.

A long conversation ensued. I, being of Irish descent, told him that many Irish settlers had married Indians. In fact, two of my sisters married into tribal families. He thought about it for a while and agreed that many of his relatives were indeed mixed with Irish blood. We speculated about why that might be and came upon the idea that much of the Irish folklore was remarkably similar to Indian folklore.

We talked about how both cultures believe in *little people*. The Irish are famous for their leprechauns. To the Irish, however, the little people are not the cereal box glitter leprechauns. They are malicious tricksters that entice you with a reward, then bilk you out of whatever they can. Cole explained that Creek Indians believe in *little people*, too. For the Creek, they are tricksters as well, although they can sometimes be helpful.

He told me about one summer when he and his parents were traveling through western Oklahoma. If you are off the main highways out there, you can go for long distances without seeing another car. They were driving their old Pontiac down just such a lonely stretch between two small towns.

Three people, two men and a woman, stood on the shoulder of the road, watching them drive by. They wore dusty clothes. Their faces showed no expression.

His father stared at them intently as he drove past. He kept checking the rear view mirror every couple of seconds. About a half mile later, he slowed down the car and turned it around to go back.

Cole's mother protested, saying that it was not safe to pick up strangers, especially when they had their young son in the car. As they approached the spot where the people had been, no one was there. The land laid flat all around with nothing but grazing fields as far as the eye could see, not even cows. But the people were gone.

They stopped in the middle of the road and waited. The hair on Cole's arms bristled. His mother urged his dad to turn around and keep going. Instead, he turned off the car and rolled down the window, listening. After a few moments, they could hear a faint keening sound. It was not like a hawk's call, more like an off-key flute. A sign.

He turned the ignition key, but the car would not start. He tried again, but it made no sound. Cole's father opened the car door, stepped onto the road, and made a wailing sound toward the same direction. He waited a while longer, stepped back into the car, turned on the ignition. The engine started right up. He slowly drove away, rolling up the window.

"Son, that was *Este Lubutke.* They tell us that life is good. The grass grows but look for danger ahead." He paused for a bit, then added, "To see one is a magical experience. To see two is very unusual. To see three, a woman and two men ... well ... I've never heard of it."

Two miles ahead, they saw a dually pickup truck with an empty cattle trailer overturned, blocking the road. Luckily, the truck had not tipped over as well, but the hitch and bumper were ruined.

They got out and helped a red-haired farmer from his truck. He was not injured, only a little shook up. He explained that a deer jumped in front of him, and he had to swerve to avoid hitting it. It was enough for the trailer to jackknife and flip over.

"It just happened a couple of minutes ago! I'm sure glad that you happened along. I could have waited an hour or more for someone to help."

Cole and the men managed to wrangle the trailer off the pickup's hitch using a crowbar and plenty of sweat. It was maybe thirty minutes before they set the farmer's truck free.

"The hitch is a goner," the farmer said. "But I can handle it from here. I'll use the grille guards to push the trailer off the road. I'll go into town for a wrecker. Y'all be on your way!"

The farmer tried to pay Cole's dad some money, but he refused to take it. They visited for a little while, exchanged names, and said their goodbyes. The farmer handed him a business card and said if they ever needed anything, just call. Cole watched out the back window of the car as the farmer stood in the middle of the road and waved to them as they drove away.

Cole told me that six months later his father received a letter from the bank that the mortgage on their little two-bedroom house was paid in full. The title to the house was enclosed. His dad called the bank and found out they had received a check for the remaining balance on the house from XYZ Oil Company and Cattle Ranch. Since the check was more than was owed on the house, the additional $6,414 was put into a savings account in Cole's father's name.

They dug around for the card the farmer had given them. Cole found it in the kitchen drawer: Sean McCarthy, XYZ Oil Company and Cattle Ranch.

Native Renaissance

by DeMetria Moaning

She is master of many things.
Most graciously, she is mother to the plains
She uses the prairie fire to paint the presence of passion for
all life.
A living testimony of seasons,
that leave reasons to keep planting seeds of faith.

Her spirit, full of grace.
With fortitude, she takes others with her.
Garments glide over her beautiful temple.
Native daughter, nourished by the harvesting of
the land the ancestors turned.

At the close of the day, her cup still runs over.
After filling the cups of so many others she is a sister,
daughter, lover and mother.
She was given gifts to complete her purpose.
She will multiply all her days walking this earth.

Ribbon of Trees

by J B Nicholson Hunt

Green ribbon of trees
Water running to itself
Flooding, freezing, drying up again

Squares of farmland
Fit together like a child's puzzle
Uneven ground under fence posts

Tall wheat fingertip height

Baking pies for the neighbors
Who brought eggs yesterday
And will pick tomatoes tomorrow

Dry wind stirs
Skin leathers in the mirror

Father's illness slows time
The seasons change
Years go by unnoticed
In his grandfather's farmhouse.

The wide sky changes color in the east
Spreads to the eternal horizon
Bringing clouds as the breeze rises

Tractors in the distance
Leave wisps of dust blowing to the north

I know they will arrive tomorrow
But I pray for delay
Another day to run my hands across the tops of the soft
yellow stalks
In the quiet of dawn

Before they become the bread of our lives.

Lazy River

by Colton Holmes

shoes and walk to the bedroom mirror. He checks out his
new jacket as he rubs some lint from the breast pocket.
Happy with how he looks, he leaves his bedroom and
walks toward the stairs. Stairs he has never walked down
before, but stairs he has also walked a thousand times. In
one of the Times to Come he will stumble, fall, and break
his leg. Even though the limp will follow him the rest of
his life, he will be able to enjoy walking in unison with all
the Times Before, when the leg was whole and complete.
He looks down the staircase, sees a younger him taking the
stairs up, two at a time. He wishes he could still do that. He
locks eyes with his Then-self as they meet at the top step.
He smiles and continues down the stairs, now stepping
behind an Elder-self. He sees the hair turning white at the
crown of his head, can see it thinning as well. He rubs his
Now crown in reflex, knowing the white is still many years
away.

As he nears the bottom of the stairs a Then-self comes
around the corner from the kitchen. They reach the front

door at the same time. His Then-self opens the door first, and he sees his mother, smiling on the porch. She was visiting on a Sunday. She brought him some blessing pine and lightly teased him for not foraging for his own. He had just moved into the townhome the week before and forgot to smoke the entryway and the many rooms. His Now-self glances back before leaving and sees another Then-self standing in the living room. This self is holding a bowl full of smoking pine needles. He is blessing each room by waving smoke into all the corners. From the periphery of his eye, he sees movement at the other end of the living room, some Elder-selves doing the same blessings, many times to come. It is important to be done often; the ceremony keeps the good energy alive and the bad spirits away, or so he is told.

On another Sunday, in the Then, before he started school, his mother sits him down and explains the Flow, and how to See it. To her and her mother and her mother's mother, the Flow is their word for time. How the ancestors comprehended it, that is called Seeing. She tells him the Now, the Then, and the Time to Come, all exist at once. They Flow together in one circular cosmic river with all versions of us living and moving together. She said it was like the lazy river at his favorite waterpark. Always looping and never ending. Back Then the concept made his mind foggy, the understanding just out of sight. Frustrated he stares down and fiddles with his jeans. She notices his confusion and pulls his face up to meet her eyes. He watches her as she struggles with how to frame it to a child. She then asks him if he knows how Night and Day work. How it is daytime here but nighttime in another part of the world. He says yes. She nods with a smile and rubs his head as she continues, saying the Flow acts the same. Morning, Noon, and Night exist together constantly. It is always someone's breakfast, someone's lunch, someone's late night snack time. She says the Now, the Then, and the Time to Come are the same. Always together, even right now his Now-self is living this moment as his Elder-self visits. She laughs and tells him that clocks and calendars and days of the week are all made up. A way for people to try and compartmentalize time, an attempt to make sense of something that can never fully be understood. She says most people have forgotten how to See the Flow. She tells him one day, in a Time to Come, his Elder-self will know how to See and will laugh every time he crosses this moment.

In the Now he locks his front door and steps onto the sidewalk in the direction of the post office. Almost immediately behind him, another Then-self opens the door again and hurriedly joins him on the sidewalk, setting the pace a few steps ahead. In the Now he passes an old ice cream parlor that had been his favorite spot every summer, right up until it closed years ago. They served the best pistachio cones, and he licks his lips, his mouth watering at the happy thought. In the Then, he's heading toward a new post office that just opened up, right down the street from his brand-new townhome. His Then-self passes a newly constructed shop with a sign reading "Coming Soon" in the window. It looks like they will serve ice cream. He hopes they have pistachio.

His Now-self and Then-self continue walking together toward their shared destination. They soon catch up with an Elder-self, in the Time to Come, where the post office is no longer there, having moved to a new location a couple blocks further South. In that moment his Now, Then, and Time to Come are all walking in unison. They are living and moving together, just as his mother said they would. They continue in stride until they reach the post office. That is when his Elder-self continues shuffling down the sidewalk as his Now and Then break away and head inside to complete their separate errands.

He knows snail mail is obsolete, but there is so much joy, he finds, in mailing letters and even more joy in receiving them. He knows it is because of his Then-self and the time his father provided the first tool that would help him learn to love writing on his own. He and his father had been on a walk out near the woods by his childhood home on the reservation. They were walking a well-worn path in the meadow, and he took off running ahead of his father and stumbled upon a lone black feather. Normally he would be apprehensive about picking up something so precious, but the year before, during his Naming, his mother and father told him that they all belonged to the Bird clan. Birds were messengers between the Creator and the People. Only those who belonged to the Bird clan could handle fallen feathers. Because of this it was the duty of the Bird clan to care for all birds and sometimes interpret their messages. His father told him that the feather had belonged to brother Crow and that it was left for him as a gift from the Creator. He carefully carried the feather all the way home and set it on his father's woodworking table. Then his father picked it up and gently sharpened the end to a point and handed it to his Then-self. He thought it was the most perfect gift anyone had ever received for starting the third grade. That first day of school the other kids had laughed at him, showing off their mechanical pencils with the refillable lead. But he loved his quill, loved the sound it made as it scratched the paper. It is that same feeling that arises in him every time he writes. That moment of Then is one of his most cherished to revisit. The quill, while no longer used, sits in a protective glass case on his bookshelf at home, next to a picture of his father.

After he posts his letter, he heads back outside and stands on the sidewalk. He is not sure what he wants to do with his afternoon, but he knows he is hungry. He looks across the street and notices a Then-self walking the pathway that leads to the park. He decides this is the sign that will lead him toward his afternoon plans. Plus, he knows there is usually a food truck or two that hangs out at that park during the afternoons. He crosses the street, smiling as the Flow leads him to where he is meant to be.

When he gets to the park, he sees a single truck idling. He orders a couple of franks with a Diet Coke and takes his lunch up to the bleachers by the empty baseball field. He cannot remember the last time he was in this part of the park. The Flow then reminds him by showing a much younger Then-self walking out to center field. He chews his food and watches as his Then-self starts dancing, his feet and motions in rhythm with a drum his Now-self cannot hear. He recalls this baseball field used to be a large grand meadow. One the Native Community Center used for its powwow every spring. Where the pitcher's mound is Now is where the drummers played Then. He smiles in fondness watching his Then-self as he dances and connects with his people. It has been too long since he partook in any sort of ceremony. After his mother moved on to the next world to join his father, he found it hard to center himself. It was difficult to be around the culture when everything about the culture had reminded him of her. Had reminded him of them. He wipes a tear from his eye and in this moment of the Now, he decides he will make the road trip back home for the next Sun Dance. He yearns for the comfort that only being with his People can provide.

On his way back home he sees an Elder-self. This one walking with a cane, holding hands with someone he does not recognize. The moment makes his Now blush and he hurriedly walks past them. He is excited to be going home for the Sun Dance and cannot wait to call his sister and nephew. He reaches his townhome and unlocks the door. He hangs his coat on the rack by the entrance. Just as he is hanging the coat, a Then-self is taking one off another hook, not even bothering to put it on as he rushes out the door.

In the Now, he chuckles to himself. He wonders why his younger selves are always in a hurry. They seem to forget they will end up where they are meant to be, no matter how long it takes them to get there. He turns to head upstairs where he left his phone. He again sees an Elder-self blessing the kitchen, smoke making the room hazy. With a jolt of energy from the Then, he decides to take the stairs up two at a time. He remembers how he used to do it for fun because it serves as a reminder that as long as he can do it, he is young. Once at the top however, he deeply regrets it. He slowly catches his breath as he walks into his bedroom, a stitch forming at his side. He takes the phone from his nightstand and sits on the edge of his bed. Next to him he sees a self getting ready to head out on an errand. He watches this self lace his

In The Dark

by Steve Gerkin

Shortly after dusk,

I stumbled onto a neighborhood party in rural Oklahoma,

the name of the small community fixed to a wrought iron

gate.

I pulled over and turned off my car.

The revelers lived only feet apart from each other,

shadows separated by similar bits of etched stone.

I was mesmerized, drawn into the enclave,

uninvited and ignored and seemingly invisible.

I watched from my open window, in the dark.

No one spoke to me.

I did not speak to them.

They made conversation in hushed tones, in the dark.

Their spirits related to each other,

muttering low in an indigenous tongue, foreign to me.

Their images danced around a fire of sticks with no smoke.

There were no sounds of feet striking the earth

nor puffs of dust from the dry-earth dance floor,

yet I saw the rhythmic impact.
I was moved and transfixed and unafraid.
I left, different, in the dark.

Buffalo

by Dr. Deidra Suwanee Dees

cowboy ride,

cowboy ride,

in search of the great buffalo hide;

way before

the whiteman wars,

buffalo roamed from short to shore;

now Lakotas wait,

Cheyennes wait,

why are buffalo arriving late?

cowboy tracks,

cowboy tracks

reveal our buffalo won't be back

Beattie Gulch Bellows

by Janet Yeager

My great-grandmother, Clarice, never spoke of coming
to Beattie Gulch, but in my visions, she told me there'd be
evil when the bison went to the lower lands.

In the chill of mid-December, with the town of
Electric, Montana's distant twinkling lights promoting
goodwill towards men, I involuntarily duck as bison gut
piles land on my truck's windshield. The sticky, stringy
tissue splatters and then rolls off.

Reporters speak into cameras of slaughter.
Their rigid shadows, spotlit on white news crew vans,
resemble cottonwoods, while protesters holding placards
of misplaced beliefs mimic a heron's mating dance.

Furling blankets, thanking our ancestral brothers for
their sacrifice, rise twenty yards away.

In the lightening horizon, the tire marks on the rutted road south of where I crossed the Yellowstone River in Corwin Springs appear as shed snake skins. I've already passed The Devil's Slide, a remnant of when this part of Montana was under an ancient sea. To my right is Deaf Jim Knob. My great-grandmother and the Ancient Ones, who passed on the oral histories and rituals of the *Se'lis-Qlispe'* (Salish-Kootenai), never used these names.

One hundred forty-five years after signing the Hellgate Treaty, our people are again allowed to resume our traditions. This includes a time when we gather and harvest the bison that have migrated from Yellowstone National Park, where they are protected, to the lower lands outside the Park. Eighty-five gathering permits—which I, as the tribal game warden, am supervising—are granted: forty in the Gardiner area, forty in West Yellowstone, and five in the nearby Beartooth Mountains. While many of the tags go to my tribe, the Se'lis-Qlispe', the hunt recently opened to other tribes in Montana, with the Fort Peck Tribe scheduled to arrive after our hunt finishes.

Climbing a low rise, I see descendants who have adapted and are re-establishing their place in the world. Near the paddock gate, four yearling bison flank their mothers. A few yards away, other females paw the frozen earth.

My cousin, Jim La Pierre, a Tribal Elder, shakes a blanket at the bull bison, which stand away from the females and their calves. Jim dances with a light step among a half dozen other men and women. I recognize Iris Little Peregrine Falcon, chief council for the IBMP—the Interagency Bison Management Plan—and Kevin Jardine from the Bison Conservation Transfer Plan, who, despite an injured ankle, sings and dances to the Bison Song. Nosing the truck into a barrow pit, I cut the engine, hoping to quell the disquiet I can't shake.

Three protestors gather by my door, and as one chants in a high voice, "Murderer!" another raps on the driver-side window.

The element of kindness is on my side. In my ten years as a game warden for the Salish Kootenai Tribe, I've found that always having extra coffee to share can work wonders, especially when I sense a confused intention. "You guys look cold. Do you want a cup of coffee?" I ask as I roll down the window. "Is this your first time to Beattie Gulch?"

Retrieving a sleeve of cups from my cooler and the thermos, I roll up the window before sliding out of the truck and closing its door. I unscrew the thermos's lid, releasing a cloud of steam while surveying the group. The young woman who called me a murderer hangs back as I pour out the first cup but is nudged into acceptance by the other two, a dreadlocked boy still with pimples dotting his rosy cheeks and an older boy with glasses and a thin smile.

Which one of you is the ringleader? The young woman wears braces and a hoodie from the local college. She stands nearer to the boy in glasses, who has thought to put a fleece vest over his hoodie. The other boy wears a thin plaid shirt. Based on this, I direct my question to the boy with the glasses. "Is this your first time to Beattie Gulch?"

Glasses squares his shoulders. "What is happening here is murder—rounding up helpless animals so that people who already leach off our government can get a free dinner. That isn't right, and it isn't hunting, more like shooting fish in a barrel. And now tribes insist on having their language added to school curriculums, put on road signs, and they want reparations. They get preferential treatment all the time."

"If it were up to me, and it isn't," I say with a light laugh, determined not to wade into the entirety of *that* swamp, "the female bison that live in Yellowstone National Park would be put on birth control. Every year, the herd increases anywhere between ten and seventeen percent, but their food supply isn't increasing. So, the bison go to where they can get food. Often, they wander onto private property." Glancing at the three, I'm pleased I have their attention.

"Then, there's following the guidelines of the National Park Service, the States of Montana and Wyoming, their various counties, and multiple municipalities, especially when dealing with brucellosis, which wreaks havoc with cattle. It's a mountain of paperwork and rules. All the proofs that these bison are brucellosis-free and quarantined for the requisite two years are in folders on my phone that correspond to the hunting permits. It's enough to have me reaching for the de-caf." This comment elicits smiles from the girl and the pimply boy, but not Glasses.

"For millennia, this area was considered communal hunting land. The meat received by the tribes helps alleviate the food scarcity problem, but non-tribal hunters can apply for those permits. And it isn't like the traditional way our people would hunt, using bison jumps where animals were rushed over cliffs. The tribe sees this hunt as a way to honor commitments and to welcome the spirits of the bison, *the Qweyqway*, back into our community."

Glasses scowls. "The hunt kills bison babies—"

That's enough. I take a long swallow of the last of my coffee. "Which is why I'm here," clamping down hard on the sarcasm I'm trying to suppress. "The hunt is for adult male bison, and anyone who kills a female or a calf is severely penalized. This hunt is a group effort. Do you want a refill before I go?" I ask, pointing the thermos toward each of them. The girl takes a refill, and I take the empty foam cups from the others and open the truck door. "Let's hope it warms up," I say, putting the used cups on the seat. As I close the truck's door, I add, "Goodbye."

The young woman says, "Thanks," before joining her friends.

Stepping carefully across the cattle guard separating the Beattie Gulch Conservation Zone from the Forest Service Land and walking toward Iris and Jim, I reflect on my earlier conversation with the protestors who now stroll up the road toward a cluster of cars. Less than fifty years after the Hellgate Treaty's signing, most of the bison were gone. In that half-century, our treaty lands in Montana's Mission Valley, two hundred miles northwest of here, were redistributed, allowing settlers to take the fertile bottomlands for their farms. The bison, on which we depended for our survival, were sent to the Assiniboine Region in Canada or sold to private interests.

Then, in 1908, three important things happened: First, twelve bison were transferred from the New York City Zoo, with the help of the artist Charles M. Russell and support from then President Theodore Roosevelt, to the

National Bison Range administered on the Confederated Salish Kootenai Tribal Land, but not for the tribe's benefit. Second, the Montana Fish and Game Department was created. Eight game wardens were given the task of monitoring illegal hunts in the State of Montana, an area greater in size than the thirteen original colonies. And third, Clarice, my great-grandmother, shot one of those game wardens to death while on a legal hunt with her family.

Not long after I accepted the job as a tribal game warden, she began appearing in my visions, where I sensed her caution and fear. In my decade on the job and now my second year working on the Tribal Hunts, I've never had a reason to be afraid.

However, since accepting the job at Beattie Gulch, my visions of her have changed. Now, she is always in a mountain meadow, her rounded belly heavy with life, creating travoises to carry her family's dead to their homelands. Grasping hands snatch at her head, keeping her from her task, and she cries for mercy.

The visions don't vary, and I'm left to wonder why.

"*Spukani,*" says Jim, lowering his blanket and greeting me with a smile. "She is waking up and telling *Saka'am*, the Moon, it is time to go to bed. The Qwegyqway are ready. Twenty of those bulls will be enough to feed our families for a year. I overheard your talking of the Lamar Valley Qwegyqway, and our reserves, and those of our brothers, the Blackfeet, the Cree, the Assiniboine, who will all benefit. It is good to have a piece of our histories restored." He thumps his chest. "Your superiors tell me that you are the best person to supervise this hunt."

I nod, but as I do, a noise crawls up my back like a swarm of mosquitos. Straightening, I scan the roads, looking for a telltale headlight of an ATV, but all I see are the three protestors. The girl sips from the cup and then tosses it on the ground.

The four calves draw closer to their mothers as the real enemy presents itself. In the low glow of dawn, the cluster appears to be a flock of ducks, but there is no "V," only the hands that I have seen in my visions. The drones taunt, circling and swooping above the bison and the tribal members before buzzing away.

The matriarch bison circle their young, who bleat in terror, and Jim runs to where Kevin is hobbling.

"Run!" yells Iris as she runs past me. "They're stampeding! You can't stop them. Run!"

Unholstering my pistol, I fire at the nearest drone, but the bullet misses its target. Instead, the machine continues to menace just out of reach. I fire again as a yearling runs headlong into my thighs, knocking me onto a rock. I rise to my knees, startled to find Jim's blanket lying nearby, but I don't see him. As I reach for it, the tawny leg of a calf stamps on my hand, its hooves slicing my knuckles. I scream in pain, in terror, my voice lost among the bleats and shouts.

"You go on now, back to where you belong! No slaughter for them! The drones were genius. That stupid tribal bitch tried to ding one, but it worked. It really worked!" Above the noise, I'm nearly positive I hear Glasses.

Out of the corner of my eye, another drone hovers tantalizingly close. I fire at it and fire again, hearing a human scream and the bellows of the bison as they scamper up the hill.

Wrapping my hand in Jim's blanket, I'm annoyed that I don't see the perimeter of the gulch but instead see Clarice. Time seems to slow as she appears in the meadow, crying over a prostrate man, touching his cheek, before ducking behind a tree. Bile goes up my throat as I recognize the terror she is feeling.

But, this time, the vision is different.

A young man knocks his knuckles against his chin—our sign for acceptance and peace—as he walks up to a man on a horse who points a pistol at him. In the halting English learned in his one year at the Jesuit-run boarding school in Saint Ignatius, he explains their plights. "The four men, they had permission. We were leaving. You don't need to do this," he says, raising his hands.

"I told you and the rest of you red savages that I'm the game warden and have the right to kill every one of you, no questions asked. You don't belong here. You're a foreigner, blathering on like that Italian I killed two years ago. Learn English for Pete's Sake!" says the man.

Martin—I now recall his name—continues to knock against his chin. I'm in his heart, his terrified and brave heart. He considers this his rite of passage into manhood, this act of tolerance and understanding. He knows what he faces. It's a stand for acceptance.

As he steps forward, I cry out as the man fires his gun. The horse startles, and the boy falls as the bullet passes through his ribs, into his heart, and out of his hip before he falls on top of the bullet. But Martin isn't dead. He raises his hand toward his chin and knocks against it.

The game warden cocks his pistol and fires again, the bullet firing upward before plopping harmlessly onto the ground.

A spurt of blood pulses from his green woolen shirt. He pivots, and as he falls from his horse, I see a larger wound gushing from his back.

Clarice lowers the rifle she found under the travois holding her husband, then speaks to me through the songs we sing to Spukani. Her voice and those of her lost family rise as the orange and pink rays break free of the ridgeline. "Rise, young daughter of mine. Rise."

Mud and grass stick to my pant legs as I stagger to my feet. Twenty feet away, my Uncle Jim is in a fetal position but is talking to Kevin, who glances at me and smiles. Glasses and the others are not here. Kevin calls to me but then peers at something in the distance. "Your uncle, I think he'll be okay. How did the blanket get all the way down to you?"

"It's being used as a bandage right now. Bison hooves can really hurt!" I raise my arm but wince in pain. "I'll need to get checked out and then file a report about this."

Nursing my banged-up leg, I walk toward Jim and Kevin, who holds up his hand. "You have company," he says. "I didn't see her until just now. She must have laid down. She's probably fifteen feet behind you. Turn slowly or walk to the gate and close it if you think she's a threat."

I sense her presence through the way the balls of my feet transmit the vibrations of her walk. She moves slowly, regally, passing within two feet of me, her chocolate eyes meeting mine.

A shot rings out. As the bison staggers and falls, her head turns towards me, and I hear Clarice's voice. In my vision of her, she drags the travoises of her dead toward the sun.

"Rise, my daughter. Continue to rise for us."

Ghost Dance...

by John Chapman

-For A. Clifford Foote 1948-2011

Hear the echo of the drum beat, see the red hills splashed
with pine,
just come along and walk with me through Lame Deer one
more time.
Past ruined streams: shattered dreams, past feral dogs
unbound ...
amid rusted wrecks, we'll slowly walk upon that sacred
ground.

The people that we met there, so many years ago ...
some still live, some still give, there's some we did not
know.
But people die and people cry, that's the way the stories go,
for Clifford Foote, you and I and others I suppose.

Once fossil fuel consumers descend on tribal land,
take coal for next to nothing just because they can.
The last thing Clifford said to me, so you know the score,

"The VISTA helped us long ago: we don't need you
anymore."

But Cliff and I were young men once we raced down
Muddy Creek,
while children cheered, we passed so near, tired we could
not speak.
We'd run out to the powwow grounds, on the Fourth of
July,
heard drummers drum, locust hummed, veterans slow
marched by.

Old folks sporting moccasins, a buckskin dress or two,
cowboy chaps with western caps ... a jingle dress would do.
With a shawl across your shoulder, gourd rattle, feather
fan,
slow dance with me my darling, out past the speaker's
stand.

VISTA in Cheyenne meant help the recruiting poster read,
Dr. Little Bear wrote the other day, said Clifford Foote is
dead.
At first we were general labor and then we were college
grads,
the tribe built its own college ... grew their own it's said.

Mispronounced some Cheyenne words made small
children grin,

At our strange ways, old long since days, when we tried to
fit in.
But meet me by the building that once was Mullin's store,
and
hand in hand we'll walk along through Lame Deer just
once more.

Muskogee Reservation

by Margaret Lee

This heavy river,

coals of old fire,

an eagle feather fan—

meager food for thriving.

This air, unfit to strum

native wordstrings,

its arsis weighted

grease-green.

White promises

its arsis weighted

grease-green.

White promises

float on paper wings

of ash. Put away

the pencils

that scribe, then erase

each portion, plat my yard's perimeter,

deny the people

called *Creek*, removed

to where Crow, Bird, Coal Creeks

run underground.

They call it *Mingo*

but the treachery is not

in the water.

Note: Crow, Bird, Coal, and Mingo creeks run through the present Muskogee (Creek) reservation to the Arkansas River in northeast Oklahoma. *Mingo* is an Algonquin word, adopted into English and several native languages, meaning *treacherous*.

Souvenir

by John Chapman

-for John P. Flavin

Birney, MT - 1970

We made our way, picking our path
through ponderosa pine, climbing up
from the River of Tongues up
into the rocks we crept,
where prairie rattlers sunned
and Cheyenne for the last century
in wooden coffins slept.

Wa-ni -de-yo-ho
Wa-no-di-ya-ho
Ho-ho ... ho-ho

I took a photograph; she took the skull,
What are you thinking? This is so cool!
... decorate my apartment back at school.
To give her free pass, what was on my mind?
Perhaps ... she'd fuck me one time,
before she left; after her theft,
and she drove back to Boston.

Wi-na -de-ya-ho
Wi-na-de-ya-ho
Ho-ho ... ho-ho

<u>Boston, MA- 1990</u>
No longer a VISTA- just a working mister
after all, she called. Remember me?
Come get the skull. I don't want it any longer.
To tell you the truth it gives me the creeps,
hear soft whispers when I sleep, Ouija planchette
moves and candle flames flicker,
bad juju, karma and heebie-jeebies,
take it away come over and see me.
Not long after she gave the skull to me
she passed away at forty-three.

Wi-na -de-ya-ho
Wi-na-de-ya-ho
Ho-ho ... ho-ho

Now Chief Joseph of the Nez Perce's
skull is in a dentist's office on display.
And Geronimo's once proud head,
A ceremonial artifact at Yale College,
Skull and Bones Society, so it's said.

<u>Lame Deer, MT- 2011</u>
At our VISTA reunion, I asked my old boss,
Littlefoot what to do I was at a loss,
The skull needs reparation back to the reservation
My soul needs some repair, I'm in desperation.
I mailed him the skull when I returned,
at the end of the week, to his post office box
in Lame Deer, he freaked.
He told the tribal council!
They took it to the BIA
They involved the FBI!
Their forensic scientists dusted for DNA
see what the science would say.
Turns out wasn't a Cheyenne at all, but
A white gal in her 1850's.
What could they do? How she got buried
on the Rez they hadn't a clue.

<u>Quincy, MA. - 2012</u>
But I had involved two federal agencies you see,
so in a couple of months they came looking for me.
After they came knocking at my door,
told them what I knew for sure.
Called my activities ... the indiscretions of youth.
This tale is accurate. I swear it's the truth.
Nothing but...

Wi-na -de-ya-ho
Wi-na-de-ya-ho
Ho-ho ... ho-ho

The Black Hills: Why the Poorest of the Poor Reject $2 Billion

by J.D. Colbert

Americans will find it incomprehensible that the Lakota Nation, who occupies some of the most impoverished counties in the U.S., has steadfastly refused to accept a $2 billion windfall. Most would say, "Take the money and run." But to do so, for the Lakota, would be to betray the land. And themselves.

In 1980, the U.S. Supreme Court rendered a ruling in a long-running legal battle. The court awarded the Lakota, a confederation of seven tribes formerly known as the Sioux, a $105 million judgment against the U.S. government for egregious violations of the 1868 Treaty of Ft. Laramie.

"A more ripe and rank case of dishonorable dealings will never, in all probability, be found in our history," the court wrote.

The U.S. Congress quickly appropriated $105 million to be paid to the Lakota. The Lakota refused the money and instead demanded the return of the sacred Black Hills. Over the past forty-four years, the value of the judgment has grown to $2 billion.

That the poverty-stricken Lakota Nation would turn down a $2 billion payday is a head-scratching conundrum for capitalistic Western civilization. But it is both readily understandable and applauded across the nearly 600 tribes that comprise Indian Country. The mantra of Indigenous peoples is, "We are the blades of grass that adorn the earth. We are the land. And the land is us. The Black Hills are not for sale."

The Black Hills encompasses several well-known tourist attractions. Notably, that includes the famous Mount Rushmore National Monument but also Badlands National Park, Devils Tower National Monument, Jewel Cave, and Wind Cave National Park. Crazy Horse Memorial is also part of the Black Hills. These valuable lands and popular tourist destinations present significant obstacles to returning the Black Hills to the Lakota, but such impediments should not be insurmountable.

The Lakota people have inhabited the Black Hills area since time immemorial. This is a region of breathtaking natural beauty. For the Lakota, the Black Hills are imbued with ineffable sacredness. These transcendent spaces, dotted with mountaintops, buttes, and caves, are where the Lakota have gone to fast, pray, and conduct ritual ceremonies for generations. From a religious standpoint, they are akin to the Vatican or Jerusalem. Would Catholics be willing to sell the Vatican?

In negotiating the 1868 Treaty of Ft. Laramie, the U.S. government included the Black Hills as they were aware of the deep historical and spiritual significance of the area to the Lakota. Thus, under the treaty, the Black Hills were "set apart for the absolute and undisturbed use and occupation of the Indians." In exchange for halting attacks on railroads and settlers who were driving away game, the U.S. government promised the Lakota roughly half of present-day South Dakota.

However, a mere six years later, an expedition led by Lt. Col. George Armstrong Custer discovered gold in the Black Hills. By 1877 a gold rush was in full swing. The Lakota found themselves outnumbered by the fortune-seeking palefaces.

That same year, the U.S. Congress unilaterally abrogated the treaty by claiming title to the land under eminent domain. This despite the solemn pledge of the U.S. government under Article 12 of the treaty which decreed that any future land cessions would require the signatures of at least three-fourths of the Lakota occupants.

Compounding this egregious betrayal, the U.S. never compensated the Lakota for this illegal taking. It was a swindle of epic proportions and one that would make Bernie Madoff proud. At least Madoff tried to cover up his crimes.

But the U.S. wasn't done yet with the Lakota. Angered and embarrassed by the defeat of Custer and the Seventh Cavalry at Little Bighorn, Congress responded by attaching the "sell or starve" rider to an 1876 Indian Appropriations Act. This act cut off all rations for the Lakota, leaving the tribe with the imminent prospect of starving to death.

Under the 1868 treaty, the Lakota had not only been confined to a reservation but also the loss of their abundant hunting grounds. They were therefore unduly dependent upon government rations which were promised under the treaty. Ex post facto, the government was attempting to put a patina of respectability on their earlier theft of Lakota land by starving the tribe until they signed a deed. Still, the Lakota would not sell the Holy Grail.

There is a popular mantra in Western civilization that, "Everything is for sale if the price is right." With the Lakota, that saying gets turned on its head by their rejection of $2 billion. And perhaps more than any people in the world, they could certainly use the money.

The U.S. Census Bureau has documented that more than 52% of the Lakota live below the poverty line. The reservations are plagued by an 80 to 90 percent unemployment rate. Median individual income is estimated at a paltry $4,000 per year. In the context of this dreary joblessness and poverty, not surprisingly the public health of the tribal community has suffered. A quarter of children are born with fetal alcohol syndrome. Life expectancy for men is only forty-eight years. At fifty-two years, it isn't much better for women. This is the second lowest life expectancy in the Western Hemisphere. Suicide, especially among the young, is rampant.

Yet the Lakota are resolute in demanding the return of the sacred Black Hills and concomitantly spurn a $2 billion jackpot. Why continue a 150-year-old fight? Why not just say, "Show Me the Money!" That would mean a bonanza of $120,000 per person. Many families would reap well over $1 million. Happy Days Are Here Again!

Why do the poorest of the poor reject a $2 billion payday? Because the Black Hills are the Lakota and the Lakota are the Black Hills. The Black Hills are not for sale. The Lakota want the land back. Land Back!

what if your history was RE(a)D

by Juan Manuel Pérez

what if *eye-stein* was
Mexica, would the world awe
at his achievements

what if *wosh-in-ton*
was a Mohawk, would the world
praise him as hero

what if *ken-a-dee*
was a Navajo, would the
world mourn his cruel death

what if *lin-khan* was
Lakota, would he condemn
brothers to the noose

what if *god-ard* was
Apache, would he have built
rockets to new worlds

what if *jack-son* was
Cherokee, would he have died
for all of your sins

what if First Nations
had built walls to keep you out
what would you say then

Dear Patriot

by John Langfeld

Tired of foreigners feeling entitled?
Tired of "those people" getting breaks?

Say after me:

   Sičháŋǧu

   Oglála

   Itázipčho

   Húŋkpapȟa

   Mnikȟówožu

   Sihásapa

   Oóhenuŋpa*

* That's what I thought.

Paints the Plains

by DeMetria Moaning

The winds whip the fields
Wildflower paints the canvas
Seasoning the plains.

I Am Forty Acres

by Linda Berrey

I am forty acres, created by the Great Spirit.

The stories that are woven into my land tell the history of many peoples, of many cultures, of many individuals. Of wilderness and of cultivation. Of money and of politics. Of battles lost and won.

For eons I am part of a vast wilderness unknown to Europeans. Both pines and oaks choke the rivulets that feed my small lake before making their way to the nearby river that would come to be called Arkansas. Marsh wrens and red-tailed hawks nest in my woods. Coyotes and white-tailed deer find respite in my thickets.

The first of my stories to feature men tells of the *Kirikirish*, or Wichita tribes, who tattoo marks around their eyes and are known as racoon- or bear-eyed people. They live light upon the land for two millennia and leave no traces of their early culture within my borders. But I feel the footsteps of their young men as they hunt deer and rabbits in my rustling underbrush.

The tidal wave that is to flow across a continent
and disrupt my world begins far to the east. The first
swell reaches my woodlands in the mid-18th century when,
pushed west by a new breed of man—a "white" man, the
People of the Middle Waters migrate from their ancestral
home in the Ohio River Valley. These *Wazhazhe*, or
Osage, (described as unusually tall, brave and warlike)
never set foot on my small patch of soil. But I hear their war
cries as they follow the Arkansas River southward from the
great flat grasslands.

The story that will dominate my next two
centuries has its formal beginning in 1790 when the
government of the interloping white men—the United
States Congress—passes the first of six related statutes
defining the lands set aside for non-white natives. "Indian
Country" stretches southward from Canada and "Oregon
Country" to the Mexican border, which runs along the
Red River before turning north and westward to the
Pacific Ocean. My few acres nestle in the southeastern
corner of this far-reaching tract. In 1803 I am part of the
Louisiana Purchase; later I am part of Indian Territory. I
don't notice.

Change gurgles in my streams, but dragonflies buzz,
cottontails scamper, and bald eagles soar overhead. I am
clueless. The Indian Removal Act of 1830 forces more

than 60,000 Native Americans from their homes east of the Mississippi River to lands primarily in Kansas and a shrunken Indian Territory that still includes me. The *Lochapoka* Clan of the Muscogee (Creek) Nation, led by their chief Achee Yahola, travel that "trail of tears" and rekindle their ceremonial fire under an oak tree less than a mile from my thickets. I am now part of "Creek Country."

For the next seven decades I encounter the comings and goings of the first Native American "tribe" to be considered "civilized" by the early United States government. George Washington, the first president of the United States, developed a plan to teach Indians the value of private property, permanent homes, farming, education and Christianity. In other words, make them "civilized." Whether to stay in their eastern homelands or because they are adaptable people open to new ideas, the Muscogee adopt much of this culture and technology. It does not save them from relocation.

As the Muscogee settle into their new landscape I find myself at the center of an immense cattle ranch, not "owned," but inhabited by the Perryman family. In 1846, Lewis Perryman builds a log cabin trading post only a mile south of my woods. His family's influence spreads from there.

During these years, the most excitement I see comes during the American Civil War. The Muscogee Nation accepts a formal treaty with the Confederate States of America, but many full-blood Muscogees vote against it. Fearing for their lives, these Unionists flee west. Pursued by a Confederate force from Texas, they engage in battle, then slip back into my vicinity where the Lochapokas provide supplies and decide to join them. The band moves east into Cherokee Territory, again leaving me to the solitude of wind and rain, crows and foxes, and the occasional stray heifer bawling in my underbrush.

It's worth noting that in the final decades of the 19th Century, a ragtag town originally called Tulsey Town (after the Lochapoka word *Tallasi*) takes root two-and-a-half miles north of me. Fueled first by the cattle business and then by an expanding railroad system, the town finds its identity and booms with the 1901 discovery of oil west of the Arkansas River.

But I get ahead of myself. In 1893 the United States Congress authorizes the Dawes Commission to strip community-held land from the Muscogees—as well as the other "civilized" tribes—and to divide the tribal lands into individual allotments. Idealists see the plan as further civilizing Native Americans, so they will live more like the country's white majority; realists see it as a step in opening up the territory to white settlers who can purchase property more easily from individual Indians than from tribal councils. Likewise, the U.S. government sells any surplus tribal land to these same white settlers.

Through this process I become forever linked with a Muscogee girl named Helen Woodward.

Helen's mother, Nellie Riley, is born in Eufaula, some seventy miles south of me, in 1875. She is half Muscogee; attends Minerva Indian Mission, a school that later morphs into the University of Tulsa; and teaches school in the Sand Springs community, ten miles west of Tulsey Town.

Helen's father, Herbert Woodward, a white man, is born in Massachusetts and comes to Oklahoma Territory in 1889 as a sixteen-year-old. In 1894 he moves to Tulsey Town (soon to be named "Tulsa") to take over the mail route between there and Cleveland, a route that takes him through Sand Springs. He and Nellie are married in 1895. Helen is born in 1896.

In 1899 Nellie enrolls herself and her three-year-old daughter Helen as members of the Creek Tribe in the United States' official roster of Indians—the Dawes Rolls. That same year she makes an application for their allotments.

I don't know why Nellie chooses me for Helen. But
for the first time in my existence I have a name: Lot 1 of
Section 18, Township 19 North, Range 13 East. At the
time, Nellie swears that she has inspected me, but I don't
remember her visit. In her defense, I am only a fraction of
the acreage she and Helen acquire, so perhaps she looks
over a different part of the property. This allotment is
listed as "preliminary" because it is within a mile of Tulsa's
expanding city limits. The allotment is finalized in 1904.

That is the same year the Tulsa Daily Democrat
publishes Helen's letter to Santa Claus. She asks for
presents for her three younger sisters, then "If you have
plenty of them, I would like a sleepy doll, too. Have you
any little doll sewing machines? I think they are very
nice. I am your loving friend. I am eight years old. Helen
Woodward."

Three years later my address changes from
Indian Territory to the State of Oklahoma. During that
half-decade, my flora grows and withers as it has for
centuries. My fauna, however, begins to disappear as
Tulsa's population grows to 18,000 and the oil industry
flourishes across the river.

Condemnation. It's an ugly word. In 1909, Tulsa
begins condemnation proceedings against me. Despite the
harshness of the measure, I feel some satisfaction with

their plans. I am to be used for "park purposes." I have a new name—Woodward Park. And a new value. Acting as Helen's guardian, Herbert Woodward sells me to the city for $3,532.21—roughly $100 per acre. Later, city officials note they are criticized for paying so much.

By 1912 the city has made few alterations to my landscape. Picnic benches dot the banks of my lake and efforts are underway to "keep down the weeds," their words for cutting the undergrowth that clothed me for eons. The county surveyor completes his study of my features in July, and the park board makes plans to "next season sod it in Bermuda grass." What does that mean?

How to describe the next decade? In one word, the scourge of my existence is AUTOMOBILES. Over the years one strip of my rustic beauty mutates into an automobile camping ground! Noise and odor like I never experienced! Even the stench of a deer carcass does not rise to this level of offense. Opposition to the situation comes to a head in 1920-21 when the park board moves to sell seven acres to the Kiwanis Club, which plans to charge car campers for their use of my terrain. The park board claims the $30,000 from the sale will be used for "improving" the rest of my land. Park board chairman Newt Graham claims, "Last year we asked the excise board for $30,000 to be used in improving our parks and we didn't get one cent."

Opposition comes primarily from a group of prominent citizens who have purchased homes in the vicinity. They believe that I, as "a natural park of great beauty," will enhance their land values.

Their petition to the court says, "The automobilists who are camping there are, for the most part, of the nomadic class. Already they have rendered the spot unfit for park purposes and left it looking like a ... camp meeting ground the morning after. The people who camp there are strangers to bathing suits; they bathe in the lake unclothed in plain view of neighboring residents. The park is without sewer facilities and both it and the lake will soon become contaminated if the present practices are not enjoined."

Prominent among the objectors, Helen Woodward, now 24, says that when her family sold the property to the city the agreement specified "that should any attempt be made to sell the tract or use it for any purpose other than a park it would revert back to the original owner."

To my relief, a judge rules in favor of the homeowners.

Helen's interest in me is not over. In the meantime, my neighborhood continues to change. In 1917, Sam Travis purchases from Helen forty acres just south of me

for a price of $25,000—$625 per acre. In 1922, C.H.
Terwilliger purchases from Helen eighty acres just east of
me for a price of $200,000 —$2,500 per acre. In 1923
Helen marries Asa Slemp, a white man eleven years her
senior who came to Tulsa in 1913 from Yukon, Okla. He
was an early-day auto mechanic and later an investor and
real estate developer. They are married until his death in
1961.

In 1925, land developers purchase from Helen, her
mother and her sister 200 acres a quarter-mile east of me
for a price of $500,000.

That same year Helen—now Helen Slemp—sues the
city to recover me. Her suit focuses on her age at the time
of the sale, the relatively small price she was paid, and the
right of a city to condemn property outside its city limits.

During the two years before the district judge
rules in the city's favor, work on my grounds continues.
Most notably, my precious lake is drained because nearby
residents complain of mosquitos and of boys swimming
naked. There is a brief effort to remove "Woodward" from
my name, but it fizzles.

The State Supreme Court affirms the lower court's
decision in 1929, and the U.S. Supreme Court dismisses
a further appeal in 1930.

Thus ends my formal interaction with Helen, and my last tie to the Muscogee Nation. She lives out her life in residences a few blocks from me. She dies in 1985 at the age of eighty-nine.

My "development" continues unabated. Terraces and a rose garden. A rock garden and an herb garden. A garden center and a teaching garden.

Two months after Helen's death a Native American presence comes once again to my soil in the guise of a bronze equestrian statue. Famed sculptor Cyrus Dallin created "Appeal to the Great Spirit" in 1908. The sculpture features a Native American on horseback facing skyward, his arms spread wide. The original statue sits in front of Boston's Museum of Fine Arts. In 1985, the alumni of Tulsa's Central High School unveil on one corner of my grounds a full-size replica, a gift to the city. It remains there amid an oak grove—a reminder of the epic stories woven into the plot.

I am forty acres, created by the Great Spirit.

Greenwood Speaks

by Angela Browning

You put my body in the river, but my spirit continues to speak.

The currents stripped my flesh away,

my bones were covered by silt and clay,

but my spirit continues to speak.

You thought you could hide your sins in the waters deep,

wipe my story from the history books so you could sleep,

but my spirit continues to speak.

No songs were sung,

no scriptures were quoted,

no bells were rung,

not a single man cried in the darkness when I died,

but my spirit continues to speak.

You put my body in the land, but my spirit continues to speak.

You put my empty mortal shell

into an unmarked grave to dwell,

forever locked away,

but my spirit continues to speak.

You tried to bury your crimes down deep,

in the red earth where none would seek the truth of my undoing,

but my spirit continues to speak.

No eulogies or prayers were spoken,

no tears were shed,

no holy bible verses read,

no flowers were laid with a heartfelt token to mourn my passing,

but my spirit continues to speak.

In a hundred years and a day they'll look around and they'll
say

"Where's all these people that passed away?"

They'll listen to what the old timers say—

the legends, and rumors, and myths.

They'll go down to the water's edge.

They'll go where they say the bodies lay.

And my spirit, no matter how weak,

will raise my voice for those who seek

to hear the whispers from the deep.

My spirit has been here all along

down in the darkness with a silent song

waiting

for the moment

to speak.

Nature's Conversation

by DeMetria Moaning

"I love You" said the rain.

"I need you" said the earth to the rain.

"We shine" said the sun.

The Survivor

by M. Carolyn Steele

1837

A ragged wind pushes at the old man's back, as if to beat him into the ground for his betrayal. Did he not encourage the people to hasten their steps when soldiers threatened them with handcuffs and chains on their sorrowful walk toward the setting sun? Such humiliation will break the spirit of the once mighty Creek people, he told them. Do not look back even one last time at your beloved homes and fields, hills and forests. Food and a warm hearth will be waiting for you in the land west of *Wiogufki*, the great Mississippi, the grandfather of all rivers. Has it not been promised by the White Chief in Washington?

He anchors his feet in the thin layer of snow, refusing to be moved even one step, and stares at a collection of forlorn log buildings that mark the eastern boundary of Indian Territory––Fort Gibson. Here and there, a window glows warmly through the mist and stabs the darkness with a golden light. A battered flag with its stripes of red and white whips about on a tall pole, a constant reminder of the white man's claim upon the land.

Scattered about him, canvas tents strain against their stakes. Makeshift shelters fashioned from salvaged wagons rattle in the wind. Such is the promised warm hearth. It is poor protection from a cold that claims a new victim each night. Plied with a meager ration of rancid pork and sour flour and weevily corn, he knows that with daylight and the sound of the bugle not only will the soldiers eat better than his people, but so will their horses. His stomach lurches at the bitter thought.

He turns to face the wind and opens his arms. Cold air rushes under his cloth tunic and hugs him in an icy embrace. "Take me, Father Wind," he calls into the night sky. "Blow me back to our homeland. I have been deceived, and I am shamed. I should have known better."

Shivering, long hair whips about his face, but he stands, waiting. The dust of newly fallen snow lifts and swirls about him in thin columns. It is the spirits of those who have died in this place he thinks, and backs away. He does not wish to die here, on a foreign soil that does not love him, where even the spirits are discontented.

The tent's sides pulse with each shift of wind, puffing in constant movement as he ducks inside. Coals in the fire circle have crusted over and shut out even the dimmest of light. Blackness swallows him, yet he knows that if he waits, he will become like the owl. It is hardly necessary, however. There is little to see––a bed of corn shucks, a hemp rope fashioned during the long hours of boredom, a bois de arc walking stick peeled of its bark, a small wooden water bucket stolen from the soldiers.

The odor of those that once shared his shelter assails his nostrils, a remnant of their living, of sickness and wasting and dying. It is the last thing they leave for those that survive. Three, maybe four, full moons have passed in this place. Somehow, he loses count and despairs that the seasons will never change. How can that be?

His eyes adjust until he can see the tent's interior bulge like a horned toad, then fall slack over and over again until he wonders how the structure withstands such constant strain. He misses his log home with its stone fireplace and a bed that lifted him from the ground's chill. It was a sturdy home bounded by fields of corn and orchards of fruit trees. He misses these things almost as much as he misses his gone-away wife, buried beneath the floorboards of his fine house. Her spirit will be lonely without him. Soldiers drove him from his table before he could say goodbye, before he could gather his possessions. Now, what he owns can be knotted into a small bundle.

Were it possible for Father Wind to scoop The People
up and skim them along the tops of trees like blackbirds,
back to the banks of the Apalachee and the Ogeechee, the
Ocmulgee and the Chattahoochee, it would not be for
long. The white settlers and their soldiers will still be there,
waiting to march them once more to this land set aside for
those of his kind, the Mvskoke.

Besides, he thinks, too many have already died on the
sorrowful walk from the old lands called Alabama and
Georgia. We are few and those who remain, too weak to
make such a journey again. Still, he would risk death to
walk the familiar forest paths worn deep by the feet of his
people and visit the tribal towns--Concharty, Wewoka,
Tallasi, Okfuskee, Arbeka, Tuckabatchee--towns whose
names have meaning. Yes, he decides, death would be
welcome if his bones could rest with those of his ancestors
in the land given them by the Maker and Taker of Breath.

Corn shucks rustle as he sits and pulls a blanket tight
around his shoulders. He gropes for the walking stick and
with its tip breaks the thin skim of ice in the bucket,
then lifts it to drink. Cedar-sweet water fills his mouth,
numbing his tongue with its chill.

 He pushes the blackened coals into a pile. A fiery heart
hides deep inside the burned kindling, capable of flaming
to life if it is stirred. So it is with the people, he thinks,

and strikes the coals with the walking stick. The burnt crust falls away and frees the glowing center. He fumbles for a handful of dried corn shucks and touches them to the exposed heart. The edges of the leaves turn black; then burst into small flames. A wispy column of smoke rises as he settles the last few sticks of wood in the tiny fire.

Who remains to stir the heart of the Mvskoke? The fierce ones have fallen, their bones feed the earth. He curls up on the corn shucks, pulling his legs close to his body to still their shiver, and watches shadows flicker against the canvas walls. But it was not always that way. Many years ago, he would not have told the people to hurry their steps away from a land that welcomed them since before the time of the ancestors. He was a young warrior then and believed the Shawnee prophet, Tecumseh, when he urged the tribes to hold fast to their lands and fight the long knives.

Flames flare and dance along a stick of wood in the campfire like they did that long-ago night the prophet rose to speak in the tribal town of Tuckabatchee. He misses this time of hope, a time when his heart was glad, a time when he sat beneath the council oak and measured the words of the war-talkers and peace-makers.

The old man closes his eyes to better see the memory and tucks his chin to his chest, burrowing deep in his blanket. Dreams are all he has left, and he surrenders to the flash of gunpowder, the shouts of battle, the laughter of victory, and the moan of defeat. In his dreams he does what is no longer possible——he fights for the land, the people, a way of life.

A mockingbird's song intrudes on the old man's sleep. He shifts in his bed and grimaces at the pain the movement brings alive. His bones bemoan their age. With a deep breath he yawns and stretches, unwilling to face another day. The tent's ceiling hangs slack. Thin beams of light crisscross in the gray interior.

The old man sits up, aware that Father Wind has ceased his rant. Outside, wagon wheels squeak as they bump along, and the ground grumbles as horses gallop nearby. Huddled inside his shelter, he hears these noises often. On this morning, something else stirs him——the sound of children's voices calling to one another. Children are the hope of his people; they are the future. The thought feeds his soul.

He throws back the tent flap and moves stiffly into the cold morning air. For weeks Grandfather Sun hid his face in gray clouds, withholding his warmth. Now, light glances off a thin coating of snow in blinding brightness, and he shades his eyes with one hand. A flock of blackbirds touch down, searching for grains that have shifted through the floorboards of passing wagons.

Men and women shuffle like lumbering turtles with blankets pulled over their heads and across stooped backs. Defeat in their manner, they gather in tight circles waiting for the supply wagon that comes each morning. Spindly-legged children jostle each other in an effort to stay warm.

A rib-skinny dog, its coat mottled brown, races past throwing wet clumps of snow in its wake. How has this animal escaped the cooking pot, he wonders, as he watches it run toward a wagon making its way from the fort.

The old man shakes his head, turns and starts to enter his tent. At first, he is unsure of what he sees at his feet. Perhaps his vision is failing. With effort, he squats and brushes away a clump of snow to reveal the fragile yellow petals of the tiny buttercup. He sucks in his breath at the discovery. That a thing of beauty is possible in this place surprises him. Does it not mean Mother Earth makes herself ready to receive the plow?

He gently cups the blossom between two fingers, careful not to sever it from the thin green stem still encased in snow. It is soft to the touch, like a much-worked piece of leather. His hand quivers, causing frozen flecks of moisture gathered along the petal's edge to glimmer in the sun. The cold invades his body and makes him shake. Content to stare at the fragile beauty, he releases the buttercup to its icy bed, wraps his arms around his legs, and relaxes back on his heels.

Nothing discourages this small flower from its appointed time, he thinks––not the bitter cold, the snow and ice, not the fact that it has surely been smashed underfoot a hundred times. Despite these things, the seed survives and blooms. It is a sign given him by Mother Earth––a sign that even here, in this land, there will be a season for the blackberry and the corn and the squash.

Placing his hands on his knees, he stands and squares his shoulders. Perhaps today he will join the others at the wagon. Is he no less than the flower? Has he not survived the walk of sorrowful steps, the heartache, the bitter cold, the foot of the white man upon his back?

The shame is not in defeat, he decides. The shame is in giving up.

Red Footsteps on Green Country (Sestina)

by Phetote Mshairi

Grand little city, too big to be town;
Budding metropolis covered in red.
Songs of Natives here long before Tulsa;
Reads like history, that fiends don't want read.
Red like tempers and embers on Greenwood;
Would you believe Tulsa's still mostly good?

Eyes of beholders behold greater good;
Just and unjust folks commingle the town.
O. Duhb-yuh. Gurley established Greenwood;
Circulate greenbacks, then paint the town red!
Red, gold, and green paradise; so, I've read;
Black folks pulled bootstraps and thrived in Tulsa!

Muscogee Creeks trailed their tears to Tulsa.
Indigenous folks forced to flee for good.
"OSAGE HAS CEDED!" the tumbleweeds read;
Only the "civil" were privy to town.
Five Civilized Tribes trekked on clay of red;
Scarlet like footprints that fled from Greenwood.

Until Kingdom comes, came and left Greenwood;
Black-owned pastures proved too green for Tulsa.
Grass no longer greener when stained in red;
Bloodshot like eyes mourning dreams gone for good.
GOOD GOD ALMIGHTY, THEY'RE BURNING
THE TOWN!
GOD has an inbox of prayers left on 'read'.

Hawks inscribed tidings our ancestors read.
Skies testify to the birth of Greenwood.
"Prejudice and pain don't define our town!",
Art deco echoes through stylish Tulsa.
Hate tends to clamor and muffle the good;
Hopefully, hope leads us out of that red.

100 years, since marauders saw red;
Lies make it hard to believe what we've read.
"Reconcile, Children", GOD bids us, be good;
Black on Black Love can construct New Greenwood.
"Green like envy; the jewel of Tulsa;
Those Drillers are Roughnecks in Tulsee-town.

Red like the Sooners and bricks on Greenwood;
Read 'bout that district that thrived in Tulsa?
My town is still Golden Hurricane good!

Heart Land

by Margaret Lee

We are coming

the colors

the feathers

the songs you haven't heard

since the cold.

Removal.

Call it a beginning.

Make an end

of what came before.

Oklahoma, this land

made for you and me—

where is it?

Not the South—no apostrophe

in *you all* here. Not West or Southwest

for, in Tulsa, we know

the month of March

from the cardinal's call,

magenta redbuds.

Red earth on the other side

of I-35—removed

from ferrous Colorado rocks.

The panhandle, once designated

No Man's Land. A sign

on the cash register

in an I-40 service station:

No, it's not *always this windy.*

The Wind clan told its story

east of here, long

before *Oklahoma!*

No one out this early.

I'm waiting for Julie in a parking lot.

She can't find her keys—like when

we were in graduate school.

Her pottery studio, closed on Sundays,

hunches low in concrete block, surrounded

by cracked pavement on Charles Page Boulevard,

named for the oilman—respected, revered—

who founded Sand Springs, the next town over,

on land assigned to the Muskogee nation.

A cyclone of lostness.

Here, near the river,

west of downtown, abandoned warehouses.

A broken-down park. The juvenile

detention center. What used to be

a Lot-a-Burger. The whoosh

behind a tumbleweed.

Artists moved in.

At the old waterworks building

you can weave a tapestry,

paint a landscape, arrange

a mosaic with Italian glass.

They call it Waterworks.

Some things make sense.

Here's Julie with her keys.

It's been a while since I saw her.

Both of us removed to Oklahoma

before we knew the dreams

that brought us here

had died.

She landed on life's kick wheel

where multiple sclerosis

savaged her nerves.

Now she

claims the potter's role.

Eve Ensler says *hysterical* is a word

to make women feel insane

for knowing what they know.

I need a map I can let go of.

The truth. My rose rock.

Take the witness stand.

I saw a woman—

she built a fire

in her heart, awakened

into possibility,

told the truth.

When you stop living

in the past and the future

you leave behind

a surprising number

of people who,

like you, found reasons

to vacate the present moment.

Together, we missed *now*

while doom-scrolling

and regretting our sins.

I changed my mind.

Yesterday the north wind

nipped the edges brown

on crocuses and dogwood blossoms.

Makes me wonder

about the Porter peaches

thirty miles southeast of here.

It's colder there, *in the country*,

what we call

living outside a city

in Oklahoma.

Worry, invasive red cedar—

let it blaze—

fire in the mind.

What is left?

Pump jacks, slathered asphalt,

cancer, surgery-scars, taut sinews

now slack, new houses

on old farmland.

Rock layers, muscle bands

swollen with toxins, original curves

warped by misuse and time.

Heartland—misnamed,

belied, bereft.

The black dirt

my house rests on

near the source

of Crow Creek

laid down millions

of years ago

by river water—

it remembers

how to feed my hydrangea,

the squirreled pecan, the penstemon

sown by white-crowned sparrows.

It holds the impress

of cattle hooves, leather shoes

of frontier settlers, footprints

of Muskogee people, Africans

in chains, freed,

cavalry boot heels—blue, gray—

bears and rabbits stalked

by Osage hunters, clay pots

of Caddo farmers.

Deep, black dirt

enshrouds our wounds

in green.

Your land, my land? The turning

that makes the sun appear

to rise and set

is slowing down.

Each repetition a kind of speech.

I am an ink-voice.

In a few decades, we will recalibrate

with a negative leap second.

Without certain satellites

we would not be able to call

an ambulance or get there

by GPS. Even now

we don't know

where we are.

We no longer rely

on winter ducks, spring warblers,

the dickcissels and scissortails

to tell time.

It would take time

to reconstruct time.

We are that far

from knowing.

I am a marble in a bowl

rolling the rim

seeking center.

If only I could read

the rocks in Chaco canyon,

Cahokia woodhenges, the medicine wheel,

understand the sun,

the tide-pulling moon.

I am this land,

this unfinished boundary.

This morning

the general epistemological crisis

feels like a grasping need to trust

a human authority over the merganser

on Lake Sherry, the prairie larkspur,

the henbit dotting spring lawns

with purple.

What hope? Incarnadine beauty

of the Glass Mountains, sculpted

by erosion. Folded and faulted

Precambrian granite of the Arbuckles,

their cataracts and sequined spray.

Bison grazing viridescent shoots

on soil blackened by prairie fire.

The din of birdsong

in the eastern woods.

I can still walk, wonder,

direct my age-etched face

toward my grandchildren,

rain down my understanding.

I am a topaz

whose colors bloom

from its defects.

Dogwood blossoms hover

near Japanese maples on 18th Street

like pink sprinkles on a red velvet cake.

Yesterday I heard a fish crow

and saw a brown thrasher

in the neighbor's yard.

I choose to be affected.

Volunteer cottonwoods

shade the riverbanks,

don silver-lined, heart-shaped leaves.

Someone wrote *Don't give up*

in black spray paint

on the 23rd Street bridge

across the Arkansas River.

The river runs from Leadville, Colorado

to the Mississippi in eastern Arkansas.

She fattens white pelicans

at Keystone Dam,

relieves the west wind

of its storm-heat, carries poisons

from the refinery, the wastewater treatment plant,

strokes the shoreline

lures me

to her banks.

Bodies of water.

I listen past meaning

to the rush from the spillway

where great blue herons

pull fish from the river in flight.

Long ago I dammed up

the rushy flow of sweat, tears

from the winding course

of my life.

Now I stand, Tulsa stands, here

where Muskogee people settled

nearly two hundred years ago,

drawn to the river

when removed

from their Georgia home.

I go to the river

when I am driven out.

I am learning

waterways.

I love the dark mountain. I love the deep water.

The slant of light when evening dies.

The afternoon rainstorm,

the sky

when it's over.

This land, its bodies of water

surrendering their bones, stories,

shells, silt—future limestone—

always a turning. The sun

rises and sets on this land.

This land—given

and taken—

never belonging.

Before There Were Fences

by J B Nicholson Hunt

In the hot June dawn
She felt the weight of her family legacy
Walking along the fenceline built five generations ago.

The heavy stiff boots belonged to her father
Too loose, they slowed her pace.

Today that was fine
She was in no hurry to climb aboard the tractor.

Squinting through her dark sunglasses, she swatted a fly
that was up too early.

With a deep breath, she took another long look across the
perfect rows of wheat
to the green ribbon of trees that marked Spring Creek and
shaded the Cheyenne burial grounds.

That would be her goal for the day
Work through the morning as the dust continued to gain
speed from the south
Cut the 8-acre patch of wheat to satisfy her dying father.

She would tell him a story of harvest success before the sun
set
So he could rest
And she could keep her brothers away.

"I Know My Rights!"

by J. D. Colbert

"I know my rights!" John O'Conner, a rich oilman, thunders.

"Order in the court!" Judge Gubser shouts as he furiously pounds his gavel. "Or I'll hold you in contempt."

O'Conner's attorney forcefully pushes him into his chair. O'Conner reluctantly sits, his nostrils flaring, chest heaving, and his steely, narrow eyed gaze targeting the judge.

"Your honor, I hereby apologize for my client's outburst," the attorney says.

"And I hereby admonish counsel to keep your client under control," the judge says.

The verbal fireworks occur in the legal proceedings in the case of *Muscogee Creek Nation v. Gladys Belle Oil Company*. The Creek Nation has sued Gladys Belle over what it avers as violations of its oil and gas drilling agreement. O'Conner is the firebrand owner of the oil company.

At issue is the sudden series of earthquakes that have shaken the Drumright, OK area since Gladys Belle began drilling. Local residents, primarily Creek Indians, maintain that the earthquakes began at the time the drilling commenced. The oil company is employing an innovative drilling technique called hydraulic fracking. This is the process of injecting liquid at high pressure into subterranean boreholes to force open fissures and extract oil and gas.

Company profits have soared since Gladys Belle began using the hydraulic fracking technique. However, there has been extensive collateral damage. The earthquakes have destabilized the foundations of residences, commercial buildings, and other structures in and around the drilling sites. Insurance companies have denied loss claims citing the "acts of God" provision of the policies.

Homeowners filed petitions with the Oklahoma Corporation Commission, the entity charged with regulating oil and gas activities. The Commission summarily dismissed these actions. As a last resort, residents appealed to the Muscogee Creek Nation to take action as the oil wells are located on the tribal reservation. Subsequently, the Muscogee Creek Nation filed a lawsuit against the Gladys Belle Oil Company and its owner, John O'Conner.

Gladys Belle's defense is arguing they have a good and valid oil and gas lease that empowers the company to drill. They aver their drilling activities did not cause earthquakes and that even if their drilling did cause the earthquakes, the company is not in violation of their lease. A still smoldering O'Conner addresses the bench.

"Your honor, I know my rights. They are clearly laid out in this lease agreement," O'Conner says as he waves the document at the judge. "The Creek Nation has no standing to bring this lawsuit as they are not a stipulated party to the agreement. As you can see, my lease is with the Department of the Interior, not Creek Nation. I have a right to drill. Therefore, I move the court to immediately dismiss this case."

Judge Gubser addresses legal counsel for the Muscogee Creek Nation. His name is Fus Yvhikv. Yvhikv has long hair with twin braids falling to his waist. His tall, slender frame is adorned in a dark blue, three-piece suit. Bright yellow Hoka running shoes complete his attire.

"Counselor?"

"May it please the court," Yvhikv responds. "The Muscogee Creek Nation is a party-in-interest to this issue before the court. The drilling activity is located on the Muscogee reservation. In addition, at Paragraph 32 of the lease, the Muscogee Creek Nation codified laws are incorporated by reference. Therefore, the laws of the Muscogee Nation are an integral part of the lease."

"This is ridiculous," O'Conner shouts as he pounds the table with his fist. "I know my rights. I have the right to drill!"

The judge again admonishes O'Conner for his outburst.

"Counselor, Yvhikv. What part of the Muscogee Nation Code do you allege prohibits the defendant from drilling?"

"I know my rights," O'Conner whispers to this attorney.

O'Conner's attorney looks at his client and makes a slashing motion across his throat. O'Conner rolls his eyes, and he slowly shakes his head.

"Specifically, your honor," Yvhikv replies. "Section 84 of the Code. In summary, this section says that dispute resolution procedures shall always give greatest weight to the overall good of the community. This is in keeping with tribal tradition going back to time immemorial."

"The good of the community!" O'Conner shrieks. "I've never heard of anything so inane! What about my rights? I know my rights!"

The frustrated judge pounds his gavel again.

"Mr. O'Conner. This is your last warning. One more outburst like that and I'll have the bailiff confine you to the cooler. Now sit down and shut up!"

O'Conner slumps into his chair. He loosens his tie, turns to his attorney and mouths, "My rights."

The attorney ignores him.

"Please continue counselor Yvhikv," the judge says as he shoots a steely eyed glare at O'Conner.

"Your honor, prior to the start of this litigation, the Muscogee Creek Nation held an administrative hearing in an attempt to resolve this issue. Mr. O'Conner and the Gladys Belle Oil Company were given proper and due notice of the hearing and a request for company representatives to attend. The company officially responded by telling Muscogee Creek Nation to 'go to hell.'"

"Is this true?" an astonished judge asks O'Conner's attorney.

"Your honor," the attorney responds. "I did not represent the Gladys Belle Oil Company in that administrative hearing. Therefore, I can neither confirm nor deny."

"I have the letter here," Yvhikv says as he waves the document at the judge. "May it please the court, I hereby move to admit this letter into evidence."

"Sustained," the judge responds. "What was the final outcome of the administrative hearing, Mr. Yvhikv?"

"Your honor, the Administrative Hearing Board of the Muscogee Creek Nation found that 1,255 structures have suffered moderate to severe damage since the drilling began. Uninsured repair costs are estimated at $35 million. In addition, reports from licensed and certified hydrologists document widespread water pollution in the drilling area. Local residents are having to purchase bottled water."

"Yes, counselor," the judge says. "The parties have already stipulated to the veracity of these reports as evidence. I am interested in the findings of the Administrative Board."

"Certainly, your honor. My apologies for the digression. The board determined that the hydraulic fracking technique utilized by Gladys Belle is the cause of the unprecedented outbreak of earthquakes which, in turn, has resulted in severe property damage and environmental pollution. Considering these facts, the Board determined that the overall good of the community outweighs Mr. O'Conner's right to drill."

"Jesus!" O'Conner shouts.

"That's it, Mr. O'Conner! You were duly warned by this court to restrain yourself. I hereby declare you to be in contempt of court. Bailiff, please confine Mr. O'Conner to the cooler."

Two burly sheriff's deputies escort O'Conner to a soundproof enclosure that resembles a telephone booth. O'Conner sits grimacing and snarling at the court. One of the deputies pulls a curtain and O'Conner disappears from view.

"Please continue, counselor Yvhikv."

"Thank you, your honor," Yvhikv continues. "The Administrative Board therefore issued its ruling ordering Gladys Belle to immediately cease and desist from all drilling activity for the overall good of the community."

A muffled voice can be heard emanating from the cooler.

The judge grins and chuckles break out across the courtroom.

"Thank you, counselor," the judge says. "Please be seated. This court is ready to render a decision. This court hereby accepts the final report of the Muscogee Creek Nation Administrative Hearings Board. This court respects the Board's prudence in balancing the rights of the individual with the overall good of the community. Further, this court hereby adopts the ruling of the Board and hereby orders a permanent injunction prohibiting the Gladys Belle Oil Company from any further drilling activity. This order is effective immediately. This court is dismissed."

"All rise!" the bailiff barks.

As the judge departs the attentive audience is treated to the spectacle of the sheriff deputies carrying O'Conner out of the courtroom on their shoulders. The sight resembles a victorious football team parading goalposts.

As they exit the courtroom, O'Conner once again protests, "I know my rights!"

REDTAIL

by Betty Lynne McCarthy

The Osage Gthedo

The old black gelding waited
Under short November sun
Knowing I would open the gate,
Let him graze the grassy summer trap.
He flew by on arcane wings, his hooves
Briefly touching ground, tattooing
Drumbeats, sleek neck, tail arched in joy.
He called out to summon
Ghosts of horses gone, that they
Might race with him.
Fueling clarity of Osage ceremony,
A redtail hawk took feathered flight
As black horse passed beneath
Lightning killed oak, and rose to ride
Air currents buffering the hillside,
Glide circles above the lone horse

Bucking and twisting in play, racing
Earthly rings in hawk's shadow.
I became a stranger, a witness, a foreigner
In my own pastures, this cathedral
Sans stained glass. Hoofbeats on sod,
Redtail cutting blue sky. Or, was I
Gifted this moment, sapient
Because I paused my own mundane
Rounds, let this flow through
My veins, pumped by hoof fall,
Feeling the spirit rhythms of every
Past horse that had run this Ozark hill.
A weightless zephyr of raptor wing
Kissed my cheek, and I knew
The black horse did not run alone.

Contributors

This anthology is comprised of a selection pieces submitted by members of the Tulsa NightWriters, a nonprofit writing organization.

Linda Berrey
Contribution: I Am 40 Acres

A native Texan, Linda Berrey got her bachelor's degree at TCU in English and journalism before embarking on a newspaper career in Southeast Texas. She lived in Wyoming and Pennsylvania before arriving in Tulsa in 2006. Along the way she worked in a library, served on a school board, led a church education program and was publications editor for the *Chautauqua Institution*, a nonprofit arts and education resort in southwest New York.

Gregory Bigler
Contribution: Pillars of Power

Gregory Bigler is a Euchee Indian and member of Polecat Stomp-ground. He has a J.D. from Harvard Law School and an LL.M. from Wisconsin Law School, serving Indian tribes throughout Oklahoma and elsewhere as attorney and judge. He and his family live in Sapulpa, Oklahoma, and are active in Euchee language revitalization. His book and articles include *Rabbit Decolonizes the Forest - Stories from the Euchee Reservation*, OU Press (2024): *Foundations of Tribal Society: Art, Dreams, and the Last Old Woman*, The Indigenous Peoples' Journal of Law, Culture & Resistance, (2022); *Traditional Jurisprudence and Protection of Our Society: A Jurisgenerative Tail*, American Indian Law Review, (2018).

Angela Browning
Contribution: Greenwood Speaks

Angela Browning is an Oklahoma native living in Tulsa. She is a graduate of The University of Tulsa with her bachelor's degree in visual arts and The University of Oklahoma with her master's degree in human relations. She currently divides her creative time between writing, ceramic sculpting, fiber arts, and metalsmithing. It is her goal to meld all these interests into a cohesive body of work. "Greenwood Speaks" is her first published poem.

John Chapman

Contributions: Ghost Dance | Souvenir

J.D. Colbert

Contributions: "I Know My Rights!" | The Black Hills

J.D. Colbert (Muscogee-Creek/Chickasaw) is the author of the gripping, historical fiction thriller, *Between Two Fires: The Creek Murders and the Birth of the Oil Capital of the World.* He has been a columnist for several Indigenous publications including *Indian Country Today, Indianz.com, The Hownikan* (Citizen Potawatomi Nation), *The Chickasaw Times* (Chickasaw Nation), and *Native Oklahoma Magazine.* He has written many op/eds and has contributed numerous articles to a wide variety of publications. Prior to devoting himself full time to writing, Mr. Colbert had a long and successful career in the banking and finance industry where he specialized in providing banking services to Native American tribes and tribal members. He lives in Tulsa, OK

Merle Davenport

Contribution: Brother Turtle Flies South

Merle Davenport began telling stories to his children, who asked him to write them down. Now, writing is his passion. He has won awards for his poetry, fantasy, non-fiction, and historical romance, but his favorite genre will always be children's stories. As a transplanted Yankee, Merle has fallen in love with Oklahoma, especially the writing community. He joined Tulsa NightWriters in 2020 and has served as the president for the last three years. Besides writing, his biggest joy is watching other authors master the craft of writing.

Dr. Deidra Suwanee Dees
Contribution: Buffalo

"A Poet with Savage Authenticity," *KINSMAN QUARTERLY* announced Dr. Deidra Suwanee Dees as a winner of 2023 Native Voices Award. Mvskoke/Scottish descent, she descends from *Hotvlkvlke* (Wind Clan) following Mvskoke stompdance traditions. Author of *Vision Lines: Native American Decolonizing Literature,* she works at the Poarch Creek Indians and teaches Native American Studies at the University of South Alabama. A Cornell and Harvard graduate, she wrote *Indian Ice*, forthcoming from Get Fresh Books Publishing. She recorded Roberta McGhee Sells' oral history in the children's book, *Singy the Cow.* An animal advocate, she adopted shelter puppies that inspire her work. *Heleswvheres, mvto.*

Steve Gerkin

Contribution: In the Dark

Steve Gerkin continues writing after graduating from Lesley University, Cambridge, MA in January of 2022 with an MFA in Creative Writing. Gerkin practiced dentistry for thirty-six years, retiring in 2010. Currently, Gerkin writes historical and flash fiction, and his fourth book—*Echoes of Light: Images into Writing*, releasing November of 2024—uses black-and-white photos as prompts for fiction, nonfiction, and poetry. Gerkin is on the Board of the literary magazine *New Territory*. He and his wife, Sue, live in an older neighborhood of Tulsa.

Kathryn Helstrom
Contribution: Little People

Kathryn Helstrom started her writing career in business, composing and editing technical manuals, advertising copy, proposals, and contracts. In 2000, she left the corporate world to become an educator, authoring dozens of curriculum articles and grants.

All her life, she traveled the world, first as a military brat, then as a medical missionary, an educator, and a researcher. These adventures inspired a passion for history and art, and a deep appreciation for other cultures.

Kathryn writes Historical Fiction, mostly about medieval Germany, particularly the 12th century and the Second Crusade. She has begun a series of adventure novellas with various fictional and actual medieval characters. https://kathrynhelstrom.com/

Colton Holmes

Contribution: Lazy River

Colton Holmes is Cherokee and Seneca-Cayuga. A lifelong resident of Oklahoma, he enjoys spending time creating and sharing stories with an Indigenous focus. He serves as an academic counselor at OSU-Tulsa and as an adjunct faculty member at Tulsa Community College. He obtained his master's in college student development from OSU and now presents to various groups and organizations on Indigenous student development in Oklahoma and how educational institutions can better serve Native students. When free, he enjoys spending my time with his partner and their three cats.

J B Nicholson Hunt

Contributions: Lela's Gray Hair | Ribbon of Trees | Before There Were Fences

J B Nicholson Hunt began writing as a 4-H Club Reporter. That childhood experience, and encouragement from pen pals, led to boxes of yellowed, fragile newspaper clippings from her time as a journalist. Her family has farmed in Oklahoma Territory and Indian Territory for more than 100 years. She lives in Tulsa and finds inspiration in her grandparents' Cheyenne and Cherokee stories.

She is a recent widow, in the third third of life, now re-imagining herself. She writes award-winning poetry, prose, historical fiction and essays, never sure if they are for herself or others. Maybe both.

John Langfeld

Contribution: Dear Patriot

Margaret Lee

Contributions: By the Creek | Muskogee Reservation | Heart Land

Margaret Lee is a poet, scholar, fiber artist, watercolor sketcher, and aspiring naturalist. She finds poems in the Oklahoma woodlands and prairies, New Mexico deserts, Oregon seashores, and inner landscapes. Margaret's previous chapbooks with Finishing Line Press include *Someone Else's Earth* (2021), *Sagebrush Songs* (2022), *Oklahoma Summer* (2023), and *Orange Persephone* (forthcoming in 2025). Her poems have also appeared in *From Behind the Mask*, (Paperback-Press 2020), *The Atlanta Review* and *Pangyrus*. Her academic research and publications focus on the ancient Greek language and the history and culture of the ancient world.

Betty Lynne McCarthy
Contribution: REDTAIL

Betty Lynne McCarthy is a product of the plains of Eastern Montana, the Llano Estacado of New Mexico, and the Ozark Mountain Plateau where she now resides with her husband of thirty-four years, Sean; they continue to raise top-end Angus cattle. A frequent performer at the National Cowboy Poetry Gathering, spanning from the third year to the upcoming fortieth, she is releasing her fourth volume of poetry in December, *Etchings*, following *Sundown Horses*, *After Sundown*, and *Real: A Rodear of Poetry*. A finalist numerous times in the WWA SPUR Awards, and the recipient of four Will Rogers Medallions, Betty Lynne is proudest of being known among her cowboy friends as the "one who gets it right.

DeMetria Moaning

Contributions: Paints the Plains | Nature's Conversation | Native Renaissance

DeMetria Moaning is a poet, writer, and filmmaker from Boley, Oklahoma. She studied journalism at Langston University and became a member of Delta Sigma Theta Sorority Incorporated. After moving to Tulsa, Oklahoma, she began writing, and reciting poetry before publishing with a Tulsa Native. Her love of poetry led her to study the craft at Oklahoma State University, seeking a degree in business with a focus on film and the craft of writing. She incorporates poetry, writing, photography, film and passion for life into her work. Her mission is to inspire, uplift and transform lives with positive poetry and films.

Phetote Mshairi

Contribution: Red Footsteps on Green Country {Sestina}

Phetote (Fee toh tee) Mshairi (Em shah ee ree)
is a poet/interdisciplinary artist with Tulsa Artist
Fellowship; owner/publisher at New Greenwood, LLC;
Vice-Chairman of the Poetry Committee and member
of the Programming Committee at Living Arts of
Tulsa; and a Greenwood Art Project artist from
Tulsa, OK (2021). He got his Bachelor of Business
Administration from Langston University. He is the
editor and publisher of RELEASE ME, the Spirits of
Greenwood Speak anthology; writer/publisher of An Old
Fart and a Thousand Sentiments; and writer/publisher
of publications in the works from children's books
to anthologies advocating literacy (Tulsa Artist Fellows
Inciting: LITERACY). He has curated over 120 poetry
events and performed in over 500 live multidisciplinary
collaborative events. Phetote is also a member of Alpha
Phi Alpha Fraternity, Inc., mentor with 100 Black Men
of Tulsa, community activist, poetry slam champion,
copywriter, songwriter, host, actor, keynote speaker,
and a perpetual learner. Ever since Phetote could form
sentences, he's been sentenced to a life of making sense
of life by translating sentiments into rhythmic sentences.
Phetote Mshairi writes for those at a loss for words.

Juan Manuel Pérez

Contribution: what if your history was RE(a)D

Juan Manuel Pérez, a Mexican-American poet of Indigenous descent and the Poet Laureate for Corpus Christi, Texas (2019-2020), is the author of numerous poetry books including the award-winning, poetic-memoir, *Thirty Years Ago: Life and the First Gulf War* (2023) and the Mexican-American Barrio Horror Novel-In-Verse, *La Santa Madre Tamalera* (2023). Juan, a former migrant worker, is also the 2021 Horror Authors Guild's Inaugural Lifetime Achievement Award winner and a recipient of a 2021 Horror Writers Association Diversity Grant. To learn more about this award-winning poet, combat vet, history teacher, and Native American Gourd Dancer, please check out his official website at: https://www.juanmperez.com

Lora Lee Richmond

Contributions: Green Country | Embers | Birch Tree

Lora Richmond is a retired graphic designer and fitness instructor. Mother of one, she is also a weaver, painter and jewelry artist. She enjoys playing with her little princess dog, gardening, and cooking with her son.

Carolyn Steele
Contribution: The Survivor

Nominated for a Pushcart Prize, M. Carolyn Steele
has won numerous writing awards, including several
crème-de-la-crème honors, and is published in nineteen
anthologies. Her writings reflect a childhood steeped in
Civil War history and Indian lore. She has two published
novels to her credit, *Spirit of the Crow* and *Outrun the
Bullets*. She combines her knowledge of storytelling and
genealogy to present programs on recording ancestor
stories. Her non-fiction book, *Preserving Family Legends
for Future Generations*, was a 2010 First Place Heartland
Bookfest winner. Website:

Janet Yeager
Contribution: Beattie Gulch Bellows

Janet Yeager is the author of the novel *Brothers by
Honor* and the short stories "Hidden" and "Beattie Gulch
Bellows." She is the recipient of numerous awards through
the Tulsa NightWriters, the Red Sneakers Writers Group,
and the Oklahoma Writers' Federation. A Montana native,
she lives in Tulsa, Oklahoma.